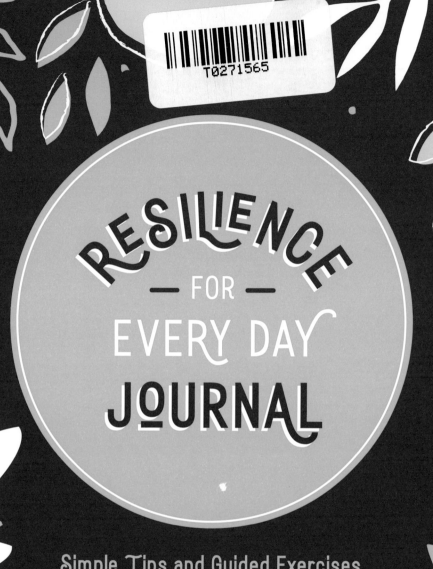

RESILIENCE
— FOR —
EVERY DAY
JOURNAL

Simple Tips and Guided Exercises
to Help You Find Your Inner Strength

RESILIENCE FOR EVERY DAY JOURNAL

This fully updated and revised edition copyright © Summersdale Publishers Ltd, 2023
First published as *The Little Book of Resilience* in 2016
Published as *Resilience for Every Day* in 2021

Text by Katherine Bassford, updated and revised by Holly Brook-Piper

An Hachette UK Company
www.hachette.co.uk

Vie Books, an imprint of Summersdale Publishers Ltd
Part of Octopus Publishing Group Limited
Carmelite House
50 Victoria Embankment
LONDON
EC4Y 0DZ
UK

www.summersdale.com

Printed and bound in the Czech Republic

ISBN: 978-1-80007-834-5

Substantial discounts on bulk quantities of Summersdale books are available to corporations, professional associations and other organizations. For details contact general enquiries: telephone: +44 (0) 1243 771107 or email: enquiries@summersdale.com.

This journal belongs to:

....

Date of birth:

....

Date:

....

How I feel before embarking on this journey:

....

....

Completion date:

....

How I feel now I have completed this journey:

....

....

INTRODUCTION

Life has its ups and downs, so knowing
how to adapt in the face of adversity is
essential to our health and happiness.
Resilience is the ability to bounce back from
the difficulties we encounter. The good
news is that, using methods and strategies
identified by psychologists, you can navigate
through crisis and overcome misfortune.

This little book is packed with encouraging
quotations, simple tips to help you build
your inner strength and inspirational
journal prompts and activities to
complete to help weather the tough
times with hope and resolve.

HOW TO USE THIS JOURNAL

Journaling will be most effective if you do
it regularly, so try to find a few moments to
work through the prompts on the following
pages every day. By making it a habit, you will
discover positive thinking becomes a way
of life instead of something you struggle
to maintain. Be as detailed in your writing
as you can; the more detailed your writing
is, the greater the insight you will have
into your thoughts, feelings and future.

Lastly, don't let anything hold you back – there
is no right or wrong to what you write in this
journal, it is yours alone so be honest with
yourself and try not to censor your writing.

LOOK FOR THE SILVER LINING

Mentally strong people have the ability to see the positives in tough circumstances. Rather than seeing the world through rose-coloured glasses, they recognize that it's possible for good things to come from hardship. This doesn't erase the hardship, but it can make it easier to cope with. The next time you face a challenge, ask yourself, "What can I learn from this? What is this an opportunity for? How can this positively affect me?"

Fill these clouds with any silver linings you have experienced in the past.

How has finding the silver linings in the past
helped you become more resilient?

....

....

Reflect on a time in your life when you experienced adversity
and in the space below, describe what you learned from it.

....

....

....

Use this space to write your own thoughts.

MAKE IT A HABIT

Mental toughness or "grit" can be cultivated. Think of it as a muscle which needs to be worked in order to grow stronger. To exercise your "grit muscle", push yourself in small ways on a daily basis. Resist the snooze button in the morning and get up and go for a run. Turn off the TV and write a paragraph of the book you've been saying for ages you want to write. Move the trickiest task to the top of your to-do list at work. By practising mental toughness in tiny ways, you will prove to yourself over and over that you have what it takes. Mentally tough people are not more intelligent or talented than the average person; they're more consistent. Practise "grit" on a regular basis. Good things happen at the edge of your comfort zone.

To practise mental toughness, try to commit to changing one habit a day for a week. Use the schedule below to remind yourself what you plan to do for each day.

	Habit
MON	
TUE	
WED	
THU	
FRI	
SAT	
SUN	

At the end of the week use the space below to document how these changes have improved your "grit".

....

....

....

....

....

Use this space to write your own thoughts.

MASTERING OTHERS IS STRENGTH, MASTERING YOURSELF IS TRUE POWER.

Lao Tzu

FOCUS ON YOUR STRENGTHS

Many people base their sense of self-worth on external factors such as what others think of them or what job they do. As a result, their confidence is extremely unstable – an "off" remark or a bad day at work can cause their self-esteem to plummet. The key to resilience is to base your sense of self-worth on who you authentically are. One way of doing this is to identify and focus on your unique strengths. Think of a time when you did something you were really proud of. Now think about the strengths, skills and talents you used to make this happen. Repeat this process with several other positive events and look to see which strengths make regular appearances. These are your "signature strengths". You can deploy these whenever you're faced with a challenge. Embracing them will give you confidence in your ability to handle any challenge that comes your way.

In the centre circle, write your biggest achievement to date. Around the outside write down all your unique strengths that helped you achieve it.

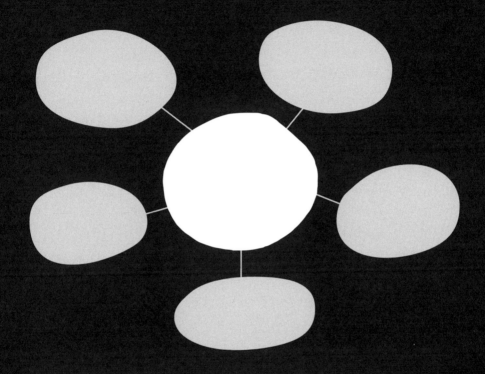

Reflect on any experiences where you have been your authentic self and describe how that has made you feel.

....

....

....

....

Use this space to write your own thoughts.

FIND YOUR CALLING

A sense of purpose can enable us to overcome challenges which might otherwise overwhelm us. It can give us the determination to keep going, despite discomfort. This is best summed up by a quote from the philosopher Nietzsche: "He who has a why to live can bear almost any how." To find your purpose, identify what you're drawn to. Which moments make you feel authentic, as if you are doing something you were truly made for? Perhaps you have experienced this feeling when organizing a charity event, nursing a sick animal, or creating a work of art. You may have also experienced "flow", which is a state in which you're so immersed in what you're doing that time seems to disappear. Look at what gives your life meaning and trust what your heart tells you. A strong sense of purpose will fill you with motivation and enthusiasm, and help you to transcend the ups and downs of life.

Use the space below to answer the following questions:

What matters to you or gives you
a strong sense of purpose?

....

....

What motivates you?

....

....

What fills you with enthusiasm?

....

....

Reflect upon any experiences that have made you feel "this is
me, this is what I should be doing" and note them down here.

....

....

....

....

....

Use this space to write your own thoughts.

I CAN DO
ANYTHING
I SET MY
MIND TO

IF AT FIRST YOU DON'T SUCCEED...

It is continuous effort – not talent or intelligence – that holds the key to success in life. Successful people understand this. As a result, they are action-oriented. Of course, sometimes it makes sense to quit, but don't make the mistake of giving up too early. Walt Disney's first animation company went bankrupt and he was reputedly turned down 302 times before he got financing for creating Disneyland. J. K. Rowling was living on the breadline before she found success with Harry Potter, but only after 12 publishers rejected her manuscript. Ask yourself, are you looking for a quick fix? Do you have a tendency to give up when things get tough? Or do you persevere and keep trying to find a way to make things work? Commit to keep going until you reach your goal.

Use the space below to answer the following questions:

Can you think of a time when you persevered to achieve your goal?

....

....

....

What difficulties did you have to overcome?

....

....

....

How did you overcome these difficulties?

....

....

....

Describe how you felt when you committed to reach your goal.

....

....

....

Use this space to write your own thoughts.

THIS TOO SHALL PASS

When you're going through a tough time, it can feel as if things will never change. Perhaps you have moved to a new location, struggle to make friends and think you will always be alone. Or perhaps your relationship ended and you feel as if the pain and heartache will never stop. Whatever the situation, remind yourself that "this too shall pass". What is stressful now will be just a memory within a few weeks, months or years. Nothing lasts forever. Everything changes with time, especially the way you see things.

Think back to a time when you felt like your problems were overwhelming and insurmountable. Describe the experience, making sure you include the emotions you felt.

....

....

....

What lessons can you take from this experience?

....

....

....

Were your problems insurmountable?

....

....

....

In the space below, write how your resilience helped you overcome your problems.

....

....

....

Use this space to write your own thoughts.

HOWEVER LONG
THE NIGHT,
THE DAWN
WILL BREAK.

African proverb

HELP SOMEONE ELSE

Volunteering can be a great way to distance yourself from your troubles. It will shift your focus from yourself to others and can help you put things into perspective. You could volunteer regularly at a food bank, or simply look for opportunities to help a neighbour, friend or colleague. Studies show that volunteering reduces depression, increases happiness and self-esteem, and boosts our sense of being in control of our lives.

**Use the space below to answer
the following questions:**

Write about a time when someone has
helped you and how it made you feel.

....

....

....

How did you show your gratitude?

....

....

....

Is there anyone or an organization that
currently needs your help?

....

....

....

Research local charities and write down any important details.

....

....

....

....

Use this space to write your own thoughts.

WHAT'S YOUR EXPLANATION?

The way you explain life's setbacks to yourself is important. Psychologists say that an optimistic (and therefore more resilient) "explanatory style" is composed of three main elements. Firstly, optimistic people view the effects of bad events as being temporary rather than permanent. For example, instead of saying, "My boss never thanks me for my hard work," they might say, "My boss didn't thank me for the work I did on that project." Secondly, resilient people don't let setbacks affect unrelated areas of their life. For instance, they would say, "I'm not very good at cooking" rather than "I'm no good at anything." Finally, resilient people don't automatically blame themselves when bad events occur. So, if they get made redundant, they're likely to say, "The company doesn't have much work at the moment" rather than "I was lousy at my job." People with an optimistic explanatory style tend to be happier, healthier and more successful.

Jot down any setbacks you may have experienced recently. Next to each one, describe 1) how temporary they were, 2) how they didn't affect other areas of your life and 3) how it wasn't your fault.

....

....

....

....

....

....

....

....

....

Fill this glass half full to encourage your positive mindset.

Use this space to write your own thoughts.

I RISE IN THE FACE OF ADVERSITY

PRACTISE GRATITUDE

Taking time to acknowledge what is good in your life can make all the difference when adversity strikes. Studies show that gratitude lifts our spirits and floods our body with feel-good hormones. How you practise gratitude is up to you. You could end each day by reflecting on all the things that went well, or you could look for things that make you smile as you go about your day (such as an unexpected compliment or bumping into an old friend). Some people find it useful to have a dedicated gratitude journal in which they write down three things they are grateful for every morning or evening. By training your mind to notice what's right in life rather than what's wrong, you'll have more emotional strength reserves to tap into to help you bounce back from the stresses and strains of life.

Acknowledge what is good in your life by writing a daily gratitude journal every morning or evening for a week.

Monday   Today I am grateful for:
1.
....
2.
....

Tuesday   Today I am grateful for:
1.
....
2.
....

Wednesday   Today I am grateful for:
1.
....
2.
....

Thursday   Today I am grateful for:
1.
....
2.
....

Friday   Today I am grateful for:
1.
....
2.
....

Saturday   Today I am grateful for:
1.
....
2.
....

Sunday   Today I am grateful for:
1.
....
2.
....

Use this space to write your own thoughts.

EXTRAORDINARY LIVES

The bigger your dreams and goals, the more likely it is that you will face hurdles along the way. When this happens, will you give up or persevere? A simple way to strengthen your inner resolve is to read about other people who have overcome great odds. From famous figures such as Nelson Mandela and Rosa Parks to lesser-known heroes throughout the arts and sciences, seek out true-life stories of courage and resilience and draw strength from their examples.

Research historical or public figures who have overcome adversity. Use the space below to document how they overcame their problems and what lessons you can take from their experiences.

Use this space to write down three goals for your future along with the first steps towards achieving them.

1.

2.

3.

Use this space to write your own thoughts.

SEE ANY DETOUR
AS AN OPPORTUNITY
TO EXPERIENCE
NEW THINGS.

H. Jackson Brown Jr

DEAR DIARY

If your mind is swirling, spending some time putting your thoughts onto paper can help. People who regularly write in a diary or journal say that it calms them and helps them to emotionally process their day. Expressive writing is also a great way to clear your mind and work through solutions to your problems. If you would like to try this, find a quiet time and place and write continuously for 15–20 minutes. Write quickly and try not to judge or censor your writing. You can write about your feelings, compose a poem, or even jot down song lyrics to express your emotions. Your journaling will be most effective if you do it on a regular basis. Many people say that their diary quickly becomes a trusted friend.

Sit down somewhere quiet and take 15–20 minutes to write everything that is currently going through your head. Don't worry about what you are writing, or your handwriting and spelling, just take the opportunity to clear your mind.
Try to do this exercise every day for a week.

Use this space to write your own thoughts.

BE PART OF SOMETHING BIGGER

Spiritual beliefs can be a source of great strength in life. Whether you are religious or not, strengthening your connection to something "bigger" – such as God, nature or the universe – can both comfort and inspire you during dark times. Make time for contemplative practices such as prayer, meditation or spending time in nature. Studies show that people who are spiritual tend to be more emotionally resilient.

Find a space in nature and write down any adjectives that describe the experience. Include details about colours, shapes and textures. Try sketching anything that you find particularly interesting. This doesn't have to be a masterpiece, just a snapshot of a moment.

Did you feel a connection to something "bigger" while spending time in nature?
Describe how you felt in the space below.

....

....

....

Use this space to write your own thoughts.

I AM NOT MY FEARS

AFFIRM YOUR STRENGTH

As the saying goes, "What you think is what you become." A powerful way to boost your confidence and fortitude is to repeat affirmations of strength to yourself. Experiment with different statements until you find one that resonates with you. For example, "I am strong, whole and complete" or "I can face any challenge." Repeat your affirmation quietly or silently to yourself, at intervals throughout the day and whenever you face a setback or difficulty.

Fill each flower petal with positive affirmations to say to yourself throughout the day to boost your confidence. If you need inspiration, look at some of the positive affirmations throughout this book.

In the space below, describe how saying these affirmations during the week has helped with any setbacks you've faced.

....

....

Use this space to write your own thoughts.

BABY STEPS

When faced with challenges in life, we can become paralyzed with fear. Whether it's a "big" challenge, such as starting a new business, or a "small" challenge, such as starting a fitness regime, the key to success is to face the fear and take action. The easiest way to do this is to take a baby step. Pick one thing you're currently procrastinating about and think of at least five ways to take a step in the right direction. For example, if your goal is to get fitter, you could begin with the baby step of doing one push-up or squat a day, or going for a ten-minute walk on your lunch break. Don't be put off by the size of the step. Small steps lead to big results over time. With each new step, your confidence and enthusiasm will grow. Keep moving towards your goal. Resilient people take action.

Use the space below to answer the following questions:

Write down one thing you are currently procrastinating over.

....

....

Being completely honest with yourself, explain why you are putting this off.

....

....

Come up with five "baby steps" to get you motivated to tackle the problem.

1.
....
2.
....
3.
....
4.
....
5.
....

Describe how you feel after completing this activity.

....

....

....

....

Use this space to write your own thoughts.

EVERY MOMENT IS A FRESH BEGINNING.

T. S. Eliot

LET IT OUT

Honour your feelings and recognize that difficult emotions such as anger, depression and loneliness are a natural part of the human experience. Let your emotions out by having a good cry if you need to. Crying can help you to regain your emotional balance as it releases toxins that have built up in the body due to stress. You should find that you feel calmer and less anxious afterward. Another good way to express your feelings is through a creative outlet such as painting, blogging or playing a musical instrument. Creative activities can reduce stress and help you to process your experiences and feelings. The options for self-expression are endless. Whether you write poems, take photographs or sketch, creative pursuits offer you the space to deal with a range of emotions in a healthy and constructive way. Find something that gives you release.

Feelings are a part of human nature for which you should never feel shame. Honour your feelings and write about a time when you have been:

Angry

....

....

Sad

....

....

Jealous

....

....

Lonely

....

....

Reflect on your experiences and note down in the space below what you learnt from them.

- ....

- ....

- ....

- ....

Use this space to write your own thoughts.

VARIETY IS THE SPICE OF LIFE

If your days have a drudge-like quality to them, take a look at how much variety there is in your life. Participating in a range of activities keeps your body and mind stimulated and healthy. A multidimensional life will also protect you from being knocked off course by a single setback. When you're living a rounded life, a "failure" in one area is less likely to demoralize you and make you feel like a failure overall.

Try doing something new and exciting to stimulate your mind or body every day for a week. It doesn't have to be a big change, just as long as it's not something you do regularly.

	New activity
MON	
TUE	
WED	
THU	
FRI	
SAT	
SUN	

Reflect on a time you stepped out of your comfort zone and describe how it enriched your life.

....

....

....

Use this space to write your own thoughts.

I AM A SURVIVOR

LET GO OF THE LITTLE THINGS

Nothing will sap your strength more than dwelling on things that don't matter. Worrying about a friend who doesn't reply to a text message, or the driver who cuts you off on your way to work, is a waste of valuable time, energy and brainpower. Obsessing over trivial things won't accomplish anything other than making you feel tired and irritable. Save your energy for accomplishing what matters most – whether that's raising a loving family, running a successful business or collecting money for a charitable cause. It will take conscious effort and practice, but you can train yourself to let go of the little things and focus your energy on what you can control. Don't let negative energy weigh you down and prevent you from reaching your full potential.

Complete this Wheel of Life to help make you more self-aware of the direction you may want to channel your energy. For each aspect of life, rate its importance to you by colouring the segments, up to a total of ten. The higher the number, the higher the importance.

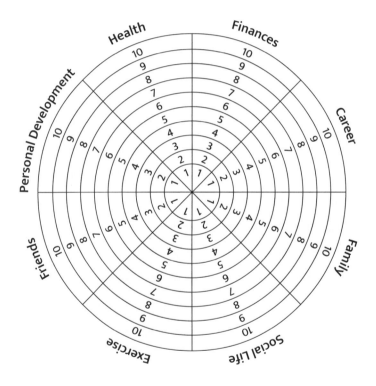

In the space below and over the page, write a list of what is most important to you in your life right now.

....

....

Use this space to write your own thoughts.

CREATIVE SOLUTIONS

If your path is blocked, create an alternative route. Creativity is your ultimate weapon. For example, if you want to meditate but "don't have time", practise mindfulness in the shower each morning. If you want to learn French but can't find any local courses, listen to an audio language lesson when you exercise. If you want to start saving but "can't afford it", start putting your small change aside every month. Whenever you hit an obstacle, find a creative way to climb over it or go around it. Never let it stop you.

In the spaces provided, write down four things you'd love to do but have been putting off because they aren't instantly achievable. Consider at least two actions you could take that would help you to reach these goals.

1.
....
....
....

2.
....
....
....

3.
....
....
....

4.
....
....
....

What is your main motivation for reaching these goals?
....
....
....
....

Use this space to write your own thoughts.

HISTORY HAS SHOWN
US THAT COURAGE CAN
BE CONTAGIOUS AND
HOPE CAN TAKE ON
A LIFE OF ITS OWN.

Michelle Obama

CULTIVATE COMPASSION

When faced with a setback, it's all too easy to be hard on yourself – but that won't help a bit. If you have one cigarette after quitting, or fail to stick to a new study regime, beating yourself up is likely to start a downward spiral that can be hard to escape. Instead, practise self-compassion. You actually made an effort, which is more than some people ever achieve. Treat yourself with kindness, climb back in the saddle and keep going.

Use the space below to take the opportunity to celebrate two things you have achieved that you are proud of.

1.
....

....

2.
....

....

What hurdles did you encounter and what did this teach you about your resilience and inner strength?

....

....

....

....

....

Describe a time when you "climbed back in the saddle" after a setback.

....

....

....

....

....

Use this space to write your own thoughts.

GOOD FOOD,
GOOD MOOD

There is a strong connection between what you
eat and how you feel. Eating a balanced diet
will keep both your body and mind healthy. Aim
to eat plenty of wholefoods such as fruit and
vegetables, meat and fish, and nuts and seeds.
Avoid highly processed, packaged food and fast
food. While it's tempting to turn to sugary food
and refined carbohydrates such as bagels and
pasta when times are tough, this will only make
you feel lethargic and less able to deal with
stress. Instead, choose foods which soothe and
calm, such as avocados, Greek yoghurt, salmon,
eggs, asparagus, blueberries, spinach, nuts and
chamomile tea. Besides giving your body the
nutrients it needs, making healthy dietary choices
can help you feel positive and empowered.

Using the table below, try adding one additional wholefood into your diet every day for a week.

	Wholefood
MON	
TUE	
WED	
THU	
FRI	
SAT	
SUN	

When the week is completed, use the space below to report how adding more wholefoods to your diet has benefitted your body and mind.

. . . .

. . . .

Write a list of some other wholefoods that you'd love to try.

. . . .

. . . .

Use this space to write your own thoughts.

CHANGE IS
NOT SCARY,
CHANGE
IS GOOD

WHEN LIFE GIVES YOU LEMONS...

If you're stuck in a traffic jam on your way to work, how do you react? Do you accept the situation and take advantage of the extra time to listen to the radio, or do you tense up and sink into a bad mood? Whichever way you react, it won't change the situation. Resilient people make the most of whatever situation they find themselves in. In this way, a traffic jam becomes an opportunity rather than a waste of time.

Use the space to write down some situations that would normally put you in a bad mood. For each one, come up with two coping strategies to help you be less negatively affected by them. For example, if you are annoyed by lateness, you could use the waiting time for breathing exercises.

1.
....
....

2.
....
....

1.
....
....

2.
....
....

1.
....
....

2.
....
....

Use this space to write your own thoughts.

HAVE AN ARGUMENT WITH YOURSELF

Just because you believe something, it doesn't make it true. Many beliefs which we have held for years – often since childhood – sabotage our resilience. Start challenging the beliefs that are holding you back. Psychologists recommend judging your beliefs on four criteria. Firstly, look at the evidence. Does it support or negate your belief? If your partner leaves you and you begin to question your worth, focus on the evidence that disputes this. Secondly, consider the alternatives. Rather than latching on to the bleakest explanation for a bad event, find a more positive explanation. Thirdly, what are the implications? When faced with a setback, try not to draw negative conclusions. And finally, think about usefulness. Question the utility of your beliefs – even the most negative situations can have hidden gifts in the end. So, whenever you recognize beliefs that are holding you back, try replacing them with new, more empowering ones.

**Use the space below to answer
the following questions:**

Write down a belief from your past
that affects your self-worth.

....

....

Evidence: Is this belief supported by evidence?

....

....

Alternative: What could be a more
positive explanation of this belief?

....

....

Implications: What are the implications
of this belief on your life?

....

....

Usefulness: Does this belief have any purpose in your life?

....

....

Use this space to write your own thoughts.

DIFFICULTIES ARE THINGS THAT SHOW A PERSON WHAT THEY ARE.

Epictetus

LAUGH MORE

Seeing the funny side of life can help you rise above painful situations. Life doesn't have to be serious all the time, so try to let go of the heaviness you may be feeling. The act of laughing can make you feel more positive and has numerous health benefits, such as helping to keep your blood pressure steady, improving your sleep and even strengthening your immune system. If you're struggling, take a step back in order to gain some perspective. Note the absurd or ironic things that happen to you. Laughter won't cure all your problems, but it will make them a lot easier to deal with.

Fill this space with whatever makes you laugh – it can be funny memories, funny lines from films or your favourite jokes.

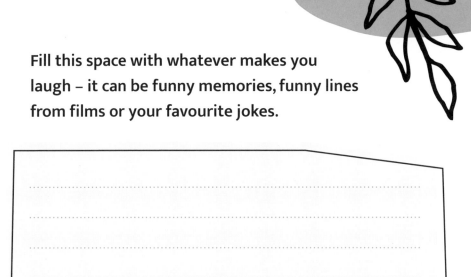

Who never fails to make you laugh? Write about a funny memory you share together.

In the space below, describe the last absurd or ironic thing that happened to you.

Use this space to write your own thoughts.

WORDS OF INSPIRATION

Sometimes a comforting or positive word is all you need to motivate you to keep going. Consider keeping a book of inspirational quotes on your bedside table or in your bag, so you can dip into it on a regular basis. You could also write out your favourite uplifting quotes and put them in your wallet or on a bathroom mirror where you can see them every day.

Fill the space below with uplifting quotes. They can be quotes to motivate, comfort or simply put a smile on your face. If you need inspiration, look at some of the quotes throughout this book.

....

....

....

....

....

....

....

Pick your favourite motivational quote and explain how it inspires you and provides you with strength.

....

....

....

....

....

....

Use this space to write your own thoughts.

I DESERVE
THE LIFE
I WANT

LOOK AT THE BIGGER PICTURE

When you're going through a rough patch, try going outside at night and gazing up at the stars. Humans have inhabited the Earth for an infinitesimal amount of time compared to the lifespan of the universe that we see when we look to the skies at night. The sheer size of what can be found beyond our lives is incomprehensible, making Earth and everything on it a tiny speck on a beautiful planet in a galaxy of billions and billions of stars. With the sheer distance of the stars that litter our night sky, we are in essence looking back into the past as some of the light we see has taken thousands of years to travel to us. Reflect on how you are part of a much bigger picture to help you face challenges with renewed strength. Your problems will become less relevant in the twinkle of a star!

In the stars, write down some of your current worries. Consider how long each one will affect your life and colour them using the key.

Five days – yellow
Five weeks – red
Five years – blue
Five decades – grey

Will any of these worries affect the bigger picture of your life?

....

....

Describe a time when you have been able to see the bigger picture, putting your problems into perspective.

....

....

Use this space to write your own thoughts.

LET GO OF THE "WHAT IF"S

When things go wrong it can be easy to let your thoughts run away with you. Constantly imagining the very worst possible scenario or outcome is something psychologists call "catastrophizing". For example, let's say you have been feeling under the weather for a while. This sets off a chain reaction of negative thinking in which you see yourself being permanently unwell and unable to work or care for yourself. As soon as you realize you are overreacting like this, take a step back from your thoughts. Challenge how logical they are. At this point you have no idea what is wrong, it could simply be you are run-down and in need of some self-care. Stopping yourself from catastrophizing takes a lot of conscious effort, but if you continually challenge your irrational thoughts, you will feel less demoralized and you will be motivated to take action to make things better.

Next time you have a catastrophizing event, answer the following questions:

What is the problem and how bad is it?

....

....

Will it have a long-term impact on your life?

....

....

What facts support your belief that this will ruin your life?

....

....

What positives can you focus on?

....

....

List your strengths that will help you maintain focus and overcome this.

- ....
- ....
- ....
- ....
- ....

Use this space to write your own thoughts.

WE MUST
ACCEPT FINITE
DISAPPOINTMENT,
BUT NEVER LOSE
INFINITE HOPE.

Martin Luther King Jr

RATION YOUR WILLPOWER

Resilient people may seem to have superhuman willpower, but the truth is that they have learned to use their willpower wisely. Each decision and act of self-control we make can feel like it depletes willpower from our inner reserves. The first step to maximizing your willpower is to look after yourself. Exercising regularly, eating healthily and getting a good night's sleep will help to top up your energy levels. If you're hungry and tired, your self-discipline is more likely to falter. In addition to this, try not to take on too many things at once. Avoid being in a position where you need lots of drive and determination every day. Spread demanding tasks over several days and mix them up with less demanding ones. Using your willpower wisely will help to recharge your inner strength.

**Use the space below to answer
the following questions:**

What do you find diminishes your willpower?

....

....

....

When is your willpower at its weakest?

....

....

....

What is your motivation for maintaining your willpower?

....

....

....

Write down some ways that might help you break
any bad habits that threaten your willpower.

- ....

- ....

- ....

- ....

Use this space to write your own thoughts.

BELIEVE IT

When you adopt a new, empowering belief with absolute certainty, you can accomplish virtually anything. Here are five inspiring beliefs to try out:

- **There is always a way if I'm committed.**

- **The past does not equal the future.**

- **There are no failures – only outcomes I can learn from.**

- **Everything happens for a reason.**

- **I create my own life.**

Use the space below to come up with five more empowering beliefs that you can apply to your life.

1. ....

2. ....

3. ....

4. ....

5. ....

What will you accomplish with the assistance of these new beliefs?

....

....

....

....

....

Reflect on a time when your self-belief has helped you accomplish an objective.

....

....

....

....

Use this space to write your own thoughts.

I AM STRONG
AND CAPABLE

WARRIOR BODY

It's easier to face adversity when you're feeling fit and strong. Take care of yourself by exercising regularly. Experts recommend around 30 minutes of physical activity each day. Exercise helps build resilience in several ways: it produces endorphins and serotonin, which lift your spirits, and it changes the way your brain responds to stress, making it more resistant to anxiety. It can also increase your energy, boost your confidence and promote better sleep, all of which will help you to bounce back from stressful situations. Experiment with different exercises and activities until you find something you really enjoy. Any activity counts if it raises your heart rate and makes you breathe faster and feel warmer, whether it's brisk walking, dancing, rollerblading or swimming. Signing up for a team sport or exercise class, or exercising with a friend, can motivate you to stick with it and work harder. It also makes it more fun!

Create a list of heart-rate-raising exercises and activities that you'd like to try.

- ....
- ....
- ....

- ....
- ....
- ....

Use the weekly planner below to add in 30 minutes of physical activity to your day.

	Physical activity	Time
MON		
TUE		
WED		
THU		
FRI		
SAT		
SUN		

Document how you felt at the end of the week and any changes you noticed from the start of the week.

....

....

....

Use this space to write your own thoughts.

GO ON A MIND VACATION

Taking a break from your busy mind can be restorative and healing. Mindful meditation is a practice which involves paying attention to the present moment and being aware of thoughts. This helps us break out of habitual and often negative patterns of thinking. A simple way to get started is to sit quietly for a few minutes and close your eyes. Bring your awareness to your breathing. Focus on the rise and fall of your chest or stomach, or on the sensation of air going in and out of your nostrils. If your attention wavers, gently bring it back to the physical sensations of breathing. You need not label your thoughts and feelings as good or bad – simply let them go and return to your breathing. After a few minutes, gently open your eyes and notice how you are feeling. Scientists say mindfulness can help us tolerate stress and deal with challenges more calmly and effectively.

Take five minutes to concentrate on your breathing, while focusing on your five senses. When your time is up, answer the following questions:

What could you see?

....

....

What could you smell?

....

....

What could you hear?

....

....

What could you taste?

....

....

What could you feel?

....

....

Reflect upon your moment of meditation and describe how your mind and body felt after the exercise.

....

....

Use this space to write your own thoughts.

OPTIMISM IS ESSENTIAL TO ACHIEVEMENT AND IT IS ALSO THE FOUNDATION OF COURAGE.

Nicholas Murray Butler

EXPECT GOOD THINGS

Our brains are wired to find the things we're looking for – so if you're always focusing on the negative and waiting for things to go wrong, your life will reflect that. The quickest way to recover from a setback is to tell yourself that things will get better. An optimistic outlook will lift your mood. It will motivate you to take action and persevere, which will drastically increase your chances of success. As Winston Churchill famously said, "I'm an optimist. It does not seem too much use being anything else." From now on, focus on things going right. Try visualizing what you want, rather than worrying about what you fear. Envisaging the light at the end of the tunnel can fuel you with the strength to get through a tough patch.

Visualize your future. Focus on exactly what you want, disregarding any fears you have about your abilities to achieve them. Try sketching anything you see in the space below.

Use this space to write your own thoughts.

BUILD YOUR COPING RESOURCES

Mentally strong people recognize they won't be able to combat stress if they're worn out and running on empty. They take regular time out to relax and recharge their batteries. Consider taking up meditation, yoga, t'ai chi or some other relaxation technique. These activities will help you unwind after a stressful day and help you remain calm during times of stress in the future. Make time to pamper yourself, too – whether that involves curling up on the sofa with a good book or getting a regular massage. Taking time out isn't self-indulgent; it's an essential strategy for coping with the ups and downs of life. Problems are easier to overcome from a state of relaxation. When we release the tension in our bodies and calm our minds, our creativity and problem-solving skills can come to the fore.

Create a list of relaxation techniques that help you unwind. Include techniques that you already know are effective, and ones you would like to try.

- ....
- ....
- ....

- ....
- ....
- ....

Using the schedule below, add one relaxation technique to your routine each day for a week.

	Relaxation technique
MON	
TUE	
WED	
THU	
FRI	
SAT	
SUN	

Describe the benefits of making at least one of these self-care practices a weekly habit.

....

....

Use this space to write your own thoughts.

I AM
READY
TO LIVE
THE LIFE
I WANT

TELL A DIFFERENT STORY

While we can't control exactly what happens in life, we can control what we tell ourselves about what's happened. Emotionally robust people have the ability to reframe situations, even when they seem challenging or scary. By looking for value and meaning in stressful events they are able to see "bad" experiences in a positive light. For example, instead of seeing obstacles as stopping you from achieving your goals, you see them as opportunities to adapt and grow. Instead of fearing failure, you see failure as a necessary stepping stone on the way to success. Reframing is a powerful way to transform your thinking and boost your mental toughness. It won't change the situation, but it will put things into a healthier perspective and keep you motivated to keep going. Try it and see what a big difference it makes.

Write down two difficult experiences where you have faced adversity.

1.
....

....

....

2.
....

....

....

Reframe these experiences and write down ways in which they were positive. Explain how they make you stronger and encourage you instead of being damaging to your self-confidence.

1.
....

....

....

2.
....

....

....

Use this space to write your own thoughts.

FUN MATTERS

Fun activities are great stress relievers. They give us a zest for life. However, with the responsibilities of adult life, many of us have lost our sense of playfulness. To introduce more fun into your life, start by writing down what you love doing – going for a bike ride, cuddling pets, pottering in the garden or learning how to juggle, for example. Next, think back to the past week and note how much time you put aside for these things. The irony is that when we're under pressure we often stop doing the very things that boost our mood and build our resilience. From now on, schedule regular time in your diary to have fun. A great way to recapture your sense of joy is to try something you once loved doing as a kid – you could throw a frisbee, play a board game, fly a kite or learn a magic trick.

Write a list of what you love doing.

- ....
- ....
- ....
- ....
- ....
- ....

How does doing things you love make you feel?

....

....

In the past week, how much time have you set aside for fun?

....

....

What are your reasons for not prioritizing pleasure?
Are they good reasons?

....

....

Set yourself a goal for having fun. In the space
below, allocate times for doing what you love.

....

....

Use this space to write your own thoughts.

YOU GET IN LIFE WHAT YOU HAVE THE COURAGE TO ASK FOR.

Oprah Winfrey

PEOPLE POWER

It's important to spend time with people who nurture and support you, especially during times of crisis. Being around positive people can uplift you and help you feel less isolated. Friends and family can also act as sounding boards, offering feedback and advice and helping you gain a sense of perspective. If keeping in touch with your friends has dwindled to the odd email, text or Facebook post, pick up the phone or arrange to meet for a coffee. Face-to-face interaction helps build trust and brings with it the possibility of hugs and laughter. Laughter triggers the release of endorphins, the body's "happy" chemicals, and a hug triggers the release of oxytocin, which lowers blood pressure and reduces stress and anxiety. Build a community of positive people around you and reach out for help whenever you need support.

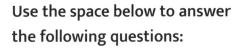

**Use the space below to answer
the following questions:**

Who is important in your life that you can call
upon for support during times of crisis?

....

....

....

....

....

Pick one person and write three reasons
why you are grateful for them.

1.
....

2.
....

3.
....

Write down any friends or family members you've lost
contact with that you'd love to reconnect with.

....

....

....

....

Use this space to write your own thoughts.

LESSONS IN FAILURE

No one is immune to failure. We all experience disappointments, frustrations and bruised egos from time to time. However, resilient people don't let failure stop them. They find the lessons hidden within these difficult moments and use these to help them overcome their next challenge. If you've made a mistake or something's gone disastrously wrong, take a little bit of time to reflect. Ask yourself some constructive questions. What did I do right? What could I have done better? What's the lesson here? Entrepreneurs, scientists, inventors and leaders all know there can be no success without failure. Most people experience catastrophes in some form or other, including financial problems, breakdowns and relationships ending. Successful souls manage to pick themselves up and persevere, armed with greater knowledge and wisdom.

**Use the space below to answer
the following questions:**

What is the scariest thing you've ever done that turned
out to be worth it, despite the fear of failure?

....

....

....

Where would you be now if you hadn't had the courage to do it?

....

....

....

What challenge scares you now?
Consider the reasons why it shouldn't.

....

....

....

Write down all the positives that could
come from you facing this fear.

....

....

....

Use this space to write your own thoughts.

I AM
CAPABLE
OF AMAZING
THINGS

KEEP CALM
AND CARRY ON

One of the most important keys to resilience during tough times is to manage your emotions. It's very easy to get swept away by what is happening and slip into negative thinking. Resilient people are able to remain calm and focused, despite the turmoil that may be surrounding them. One of the best ways to build this skill is to practise remaining calm and focused in everyday situations. If you practise on the little things, calmness will become a habit that will kick in when you need it most. The next time you're stuck in a traffic jam or your bag breaks and empties your shopping all over the floor, try breathing in deeply through your nose, and holding it for a moment before breathing out of your mouth. By doing this for a few minutes you should find yourself feeling calmer and more relaxed. The regular practice of yoga, meditation or mindfulness can also help you with this.

When you are struggling to manage your emotions, step back from the situation and try to remember life's positives by asking yourself the following:

Name three positive things that happened to you today.
1.
2.
3.

Name three things that you did for someone else today.
1.
2.
3.

Name three ways you've been productive today.
1.
2.
3.

Name three things you are grateful for today.
1.
2.
3.

Use this space to write your own thoughts.

TIME FOR BED

Sleep keeps you mentally and physically strong. Just one night of bad sleep can cause you to feel negative, irritable and more easily overwhelmed the next day. Most adults need at least 7–8 hours' sleep a night, but everyone is different. If you wake up feeling refreshed, you're probably getting enough sleep. If you're not getting enough sleep, the following tips will help: take time to unwind before bed – dim the lights, listen to calming music, have a bath or meditate. Turn your bedroom into a relaxing space by removing any clutter and painting the walls a neutral, calming colour. Ensure your bedroom is as dark as possible – ban electronic gadgets and consider getting thicker curtains or blackout blinds. If your mind is racing, try jotting down your thoughts in a diary. These simple actions can turn your bedroom into a peaceful sanctuary and encourage a better night's sleep.

**What are your three favourite things
about your bedroom?**

1.
....
2.
....
3.
....

**Write down some actions you could take to turn your
bedroom into a more peaceful sanctuary.**

-
....
-
....
-
....
-
....
-
....
-
....

Try making a couple of the above changes.
Describe the difference they have made.

....
....
....
....
....

Use this space to write your own thoughts.

WITH THE NEW DAY COMES NEW STRENGTH AND NEW THOUGHTS.

Eleanor Roosevelt

FINAL WORD

Congratulations for completing this resilience journal. The ability to adapt is key to your health and happiness, so continue to use the tools within this book to navigate your way through any setbacks. True resilience comes from basing your sense of self-worth on who you authentically are. Focus on your unique strengths while reminding yourself of all the times you've succeeded in overcoming adversity. Embracing these strengths, while acknowledging and working at overcoming weaknesses, is essential for providing you with the ability to handle future challenges.

If you find yourself slipping back into negativity, revisit the key points in your journal where you identified what gives you a strong sense of purpose and reflect on everything you are grateful for in your life. What seems insurmountable now will be just a memory within a few weeks, months or years. Take time to relax and recharge your batteries and, most importantly, be kind to yourself.

Happiness for Every Day Journal

Simple Tips and Guided
Exercises to Help You Find Joy

Paperback

ISBN: 978-1-80007-832-1

Mindfulness for Every Day Journal

Simple Tips and Guided Exercises
to Help You Live in the Moment

Paperback

ISBN: 978-1-80007-835-2

Positivity for Every Day Journal

Simple Tips and Guided
Exercises to Help You Look
on the Bright Side

Paperback

ISBN: 978-1-80007-833-8

Have you enjoyed this book?
If so, find us on Facebook at **Summersdale Publishers**, on Twitter at **@Summersdale** and on Instagram at **@summersdalebooks** and get in touch. We'd love to hear from you!

www.summersdale.com

IMAGE CREDITS